THE LEWIS AND CLARK EXPEDITION

O.C.SELTZER.

Turning Points in American History

THE LEWIS AND CLARK EXPEDITION

Patrick McGrath

Silver Burdett Company, Morristown, New Jersey

Cincinnati; Glenview, Ill.; San Carlos, Calif.;
Dallas; Atlanta; Agincourt, Ontario

Acknowledgements

We would like to thank the following people for reviewing the manuscript and for their guidance and helpful suggestions: David Williams, Professor of History, California State University; Craighton Hippenhammer, Assistant Coordinator and Children's Service Manager, Cuyahoga Co. Public Library, Cleveland, Ohio.

Cover: Detail from E. S. Paxson's painting of the expedition at Three Forks courtesy of the Montana Historical Society

Title page: O.C. Seltzer's painting of Lewis and Clark at the Great Falls of the Missouri courtesy of the Thomas Gilcrease Institute of American History and Art, Tulsa, Oklahoma

Contents page: Relief, by Karl Bitter, showing the signing of the Louisiana Purchase courtesy of the Missouri Historical Society

Page 47: Paxson's painting of the expedition at Three Forks courtesy of the Montana Historical Society

Page 57: Clark's drawings of Chinook Indians courtesy of the Missouri Historical Society

Library of Congress Cataloging in Publication Data

McGrath, Patrick, 1950–
   The Lewis and Clark expedition.

   (Turning points in American history)
   "Created by Media Projects, Inc."—T. p. verso.
   Bibliography: p.
   Includes index.
   Summary: An account of the 1804–1806 Lewis and Clark Expedition which explored the unknown Louisiana Purchase territory and the Pacific Northwest from St. Louis to the mouth of the Columbia River.
   1. Lewis and Clark Expedition (1804–1806)—Juvenile literature. [1. Lewis and Clark Expedition (1804–1806)] I. Title. II. Series.
F592.7.M34 1985 917.8'042 84–40381

ISBN 0-382-06828-9 (lib. bdg.)

 Created by Media Projects, Inc.

Series design by Bruce Glassman
Ellen Coffey, Project Manager
Frank L. Kurtz, Project Editor
Jeffrey Woldt, Photo Research Editor

Published simultaneously in Canada by GLC/Silver Burdett Publishers

Manufactured in the United States of America

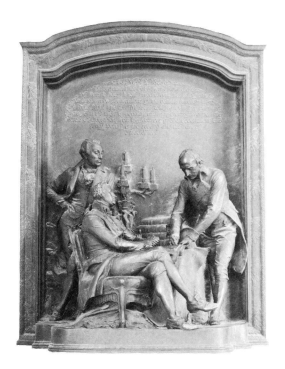

CONTENTS

INTRODUCTION

THE MOUNTAIN BARRIER

On a hot August morning in 1805, a scouting party of four sunburned men trekked wearily along a wide, level valley in the foothills of the Rocky Mountains. The men were spaced wide apart but moved up the valley abreast of one another. Each was dressed in buckskin, and carried a pack and a rifle. Their leader was a tough young army captain named Meriwether Lewis. As he trudged along, he glanced anxiously at the towering mountains to the west, the peaks of which formed an unbroken chain running from north to south. The expedition had to get over those mountains before the fall snows came. But the mountains could not be crossed without horses—and the Indians with horses to sell would not show themselves.

The four explorers plodded on up the

Meriwether Lewis posed for this portrait by the French artist Charles de Saint-Mémin not long after the expedition's return to St. Louis. The fur shawl was a gift from the Shoshoni.

valley. Lewis was in the center, with a man named McNeal. The other two men, George Drouilliard and John Shields, were off to either side, well out of earshot. For some days now there had been signs of Shoshoni Indians in the area. The Shoshoni had horses to sell, and knew the mountains well. They could guide the expedition through the Rockies. But they were a people who had never met white men, and they kept to the hills. Lewis knew that if he did not make contact with them soon, the expedition might have to turn back.

He did not like to think of that. They had already been under way a full year and had come up the Missouri River some three thousand miles. If they succeeded in reaching the Pacific, they would be the first white men to cross the North American continent. It was unthinkable to turn back now.

Suddenly, far ahead, a horseman appeared. He was riding toward them along a creek. Lewis, in his excitement, dropped his pocket telescope. But he had seen enough to know that the stranger was a Shoshoni, and that he was mounted on a fine horse. Lewis took a blanket from his pack and made the peace signal by flapping it three times in the air, then laying it flat on the ground. The Indian stopped, still some distance away. Lewis held up some presents, to show his friendly intentions.

But the Indian was suspicious. He feared some trickery from these strangers. He was looking not at Lewis but at Drouilliard and Shields, who were still advancing up the valley. Lewis saw what was happening and signaled desperately to his men to stop. If this Indian told the rest of his people that these men were not to be trusted, the Shoshoni would simply vanish into the mountains. Then there would be no buying horses. In a month the fall snows would come, and the Rockies would be impassable.

Drouilliard saw the signal, stopped, and laid down his gun. But Shields kept on going. The Indian eyed him very warily and began to edge away.

"Tab-ba-bone!" Lewis cried, using the word he knew meant "white man." He pulled up his sleeve to show that he was no enemy but a white man who had come in peace. But the lone horseman was still watching Shields. Suddenly, he seemed to make up his mind. He turned his horse, jumped the creek, and galloped off into the trees. He was gone.

Lewis called his men to him and furiously dressed them down. They'd scared away the only Indian they'd seen in days.

But there was nothing to be done now. The chance was missed. They built a fire and had breakfast, then took up the trail again. Lewis could only hope that he'd be given another chance to make contact with the wary Shoshoni.

Captain William Clark, meanwhile, was coming upstream with the rest of the expedition. Clark was a big, strong, red-haired man of thirty-four, with a cheerful, outgoing personality. In many ways he was the opposite of his friend Lewis, who was a quieter, somewhat moody man. Clark, like Lewis, had been a professional soldier on the frontier for some time. He knew Indians, and he knew how to take care of himself in the wilderness. When Lewis had asked him to join an expedition up the Missouri and over the mountains to the Pacific, he had jumped at the chance. They would share the command, Lewis had assured his friend. It would be the "Lewis and Clark expedition."

They had left St. Louis in the summer of 1804 with a group of tough young soldiers and spent a year coming up the Missouri River. By the summer of 1805, they'd reached the foothills of the Rockies, and the going had become very rough. For the river here, in what today is the western part of Montana, was so swift that the men could no longer paddle the expedition's heavily laden canoes. They'd had to pole them along, or tow them from the bank. Sometimes they'd had to wade through the water and drag them.

To make matters worse, some of the men had fallen ill. Clark himself had a badly infected ankle, from an insect bite,

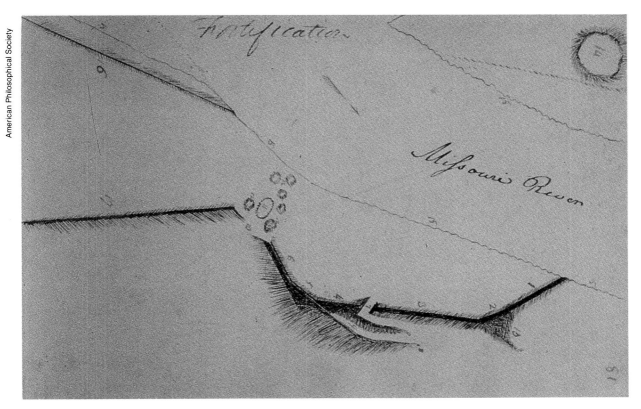

Drawing of an Indian fortification on the Missouri River, from the journals of Lewis and Clark

and couldn't walk. Others had been hurt in falls or were afflicted with boils. One man had dysentery and another had been badly injured when his canoe overturned. All in all, the expedition was in poor shape as it approached its most difficult challenge.

So Lewis and three of the most reliable men had set off in advance of the main party to make contact with the Shoshoni. It was soon after this that the chance had been missed with the lone horseman. They then followed the trail up the valley and, the next day, veered west through a mountain pass. Lewis suspected that they were on an Indian road and that sooner or

later it would bring them to a village.

Sure enough, on the fourth day since they'd left the rest of the party, Lewis and the others suddenly came upon three Shoshoni women in a ravine. One woman fled, but the other two bowed their heads as if they expected to be executed. Instead, Lewis gave them presents, and then painted their faces bright red—a sign he came in peace. The women promptly indicated that they would take him and his men to the Shoshoni camp.

Lewis must surely have thought that now, at last, he was getting close to his goal. But the happy group had gone only two miles when they heard a thundering sound. There suddenly appeared a party of sixty Shoshoni warriors, armed for battle, galloping straight toward them.

Lewis told the others to stop, and went forward alone to meet the Shoshoni. By this time he had had many meetings with chiefs of various tribes, and he knew how to act. He watched as the chief dismounted and spoke to the women. The chief then came up to Lewis and embraced him. He was satisfied that the white men came in peace. Soon a peace pipe was being passed around, and Lewis gave the chief a flag and some small objects symbolic of friendship. The white men were then led to the village, made comfortable in a tepee, and a celebration followed. Lewis was so tired that before long he crept off to sleep.

Still, his problems were far from over. The next day, he learned that the Shoshoni had a herd of seven hundred

This Plains Indian calumet, or ceremonial peace pipe, was among the many artifacts sent east by Lewis and Clark in the spring of 1805.

Peabody Museum, Harvard University

horses. Surely they could provide what the expedition needed. He was impatient now to return to Clark and the others, along with some tribesmen, and begin trading. But the Shoshoni became suspicious when he asked them to ride back to the river with him. They thought that Lewis and his men were trying to draw them into a trap set by their old enemies, the Blackfoot Indians. They were reluctant to leave their village. Finally, when Lewis hinted that the chief was not brave enough to come with him to the river, the chief climbed onto his horse and was joined by six or eight tribesmen.

They left the Shoshoni camp and set off toward the river, which was several days' journey away. On the way Drouilliard shot several deer, and Lewis shared the venison with the hungry Indians. Even so, the Shoshoni were expecting a trap. By the time they were close to the place on the river where Lewis expected the expedition to be, the Indians had become very anxious. As they approached, several Shoshoni hid in the undergrowth, and others insisted that Lewis remove his cocked hat so that any Blackfoot warriors lying in wait could not recognize him. Then, to his dismay, Lewis realized that Clark and the others had not arrived yet. This was a bad blow, for he had assured the Indians that there would be food and gifts when they met his friends. The Indians were suspicious already. What would they do when they found out that Lewis's promises were empty?

1

LOOKING WEST

As Lewis and Clark were edging deeper into the wilds of the Northwest, their commander in chief, Thomas Jefferson, eagerly awaited news of them in Washington. Philosopher, lawyer, scientist, architect, inventor, Jefferson was a man of extraordinary abilities. Now, as the third president of the United States, he was eager to ensure a bright future for the young republic.

The United States at this time consisted only of lands east of the Mississippi River. France and Spain controlled lands west of the Mississippi as far as the Rocky Mountains—the vast area known as the Louisiana Territory—and England and Spain between them claimed the rest of the continent.

But many in the young republic believed that the States should eventually consist of all lands from the Atlantic to the

Thomas Jefferson
(painting by Charles Wilson Peale)

Pacific, and the most passionate in this belief was Thomas Jefferson. The best way to claim the land, he thought, was to send out an exploring party to report on what was there. The report would fire the imaginations of adventurous Americans, and a wave of settlement would follow.

Long before he became president, Jefferson had been interested in the Northwest, for he understood its great commercial importance. In 1804, however, there were no accurate maps of the region. It was known that the Missouri had its source in the Rockies, but what lay beyond was uncertain. Many people believed that a mountain lake connected the Missouri to a great river flowing west to the Pacific. Others thought that a short land passage connected the two rivers. Whichever was correct, if Americans could control the route, Britain's dominant position in the fur trade in the Northwest would be greatly weakened. Not only that, but a shortcut to the markets of the

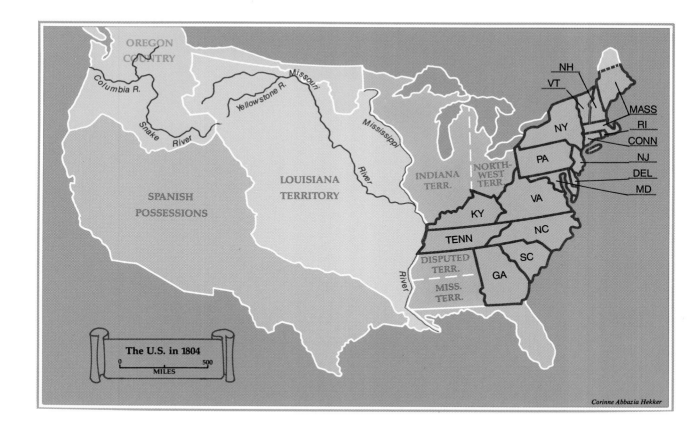

OREGON COUNTRY

Columbia R.

Snake River

Yellowstone R.

Missouri

Mississippi

River

SPANISH POSSESSIONS

LOUISIANA TERRITORY

INDIANA TERR.

NORTH-WEST TERR.

KY

TENN

DISPUTED TERR.

MISS. TERR.

GA

SC

NC

VA

PA

NY

VT

NH

MASS

RI

CONN

NJ

DEL

MD

The U.S. in 1804

0   500
MILES

Corinne Abbazia Hekker

Pacific and the Orient would be opened up to American industries on the East Coast. And goods from the Orient, bound for Europe, would be carried across the United States to its eastern ports, to be shipped from there across the Atlantic. If such a waterway existed, the young republic would quickly become a much more powerful nation.

Jefferson dreamed of organizing the expedition that would find the fabled "Northwest Passage" and claim it for the States. When he became president, in 1801, he was in a position to make that dream a reality. The first problem was

finding someone capable of heading the expedition, a person who could do more than just lead an adventurous trek to the West Coast. For one thing, the expedition would have to establish good relations with the Indians. If the country were to expand westward, the Indians must be persuaded to give up their old ways and become peaceful farmers. This was how Jefferson imagined them fitting into the white man's civilization. Whoever led the expedition must be able to handle this delicate task of diplomacy.

Also, Jefferson had a scientist's passionate curiosity about the natural history of the vast unexplored region of the upper Missouri and the lands west of it. There were dozens of questions he wanted answered about the flora and fauna of these parts, about the ways of the Indian tribes who lived here, about the soil, the climate. All in all, then, the leader of Jefferson's expedition would have to be a person of many talents: explorer, scientist, diplomat.

The president remembered a young man who had asked to join an expedition to the Northwest in 1792. Like several other planned expeditions, this one didn't materialize. But Jefferson had been impressed by the young man. His name was Meriwether Lewis, and he came from Albemarle County, in Virginia, where his family lived not far from Jefferson's.

Meriwether Lewis was the eldest son in his family, and he left school at fifteen to work the family land. He loved the outdoors from his earliest years, and even at age eight he would go out alone, in the depth of winter, on hunting expeditions with his dogs.

He joined the army after the 1792 expedition fell through and rose to the rank of captain. During these years he spent much time on the frontier and had many dealings with Indians. Jefferson was very fond of his fellow Virginian, and in 1801 he appointed Lewis his personal secretary.

By 1803 Jefferson was satisfied that Lewis had the makings of the explorer-scientist-diplomat he needed for his expedition. The president then began to attend to the political aspects of the project. He had to be careful here, for France,

Meriwether Lewis
(painting by Charles Wilson Peale)

under Napoleon, held most of the land west of the Mississippi to the Rockies and wouldn't like the idea of U.S. exploration of the Louisiana Territory. Even so, Jefferson persuaded Congress to approve the expedition, and even to appropriate $2,500 to cover its expenses. As it turned out, the final cost was almost twenty times that amount, about $40,000.

As for problems with France, they never materialized. A few months before the expedition left, the United States bought the Louisiana Territory for $15 million. The Louisiana Purchase, as it was called, opened the way for an expedition that would be within U.S. territory until it reached the Rockies. Jefferson had done his part; now it was up to Lewis.

him. If you can not learn that Conner has gone on to Mapac Kaskaskais or Illinois, (which are the place I appointed for his joining me) I think it will be best for you to hire a man to go to the Delleware Town and enquire after him, you may offer him three hundred dollars a year and find him provi:sions and clothing — should he be at the Deleware town and be willing to engage on these terms he had better com on immiedately and join us at Louisvi he is a trader among the Indians and I think he told me he lived _on White river_ at the nearest Dellaware tow to Fort Hamilton and distant from that pe about 24 miles. ————

The session of Louisiana is now no on the 14th. of July the President recieved the treaty fro Paris, by which France has ceded to the U States, Lou :siana according to the bounds to which she had a wre price 11¼ Millions of dollars, besides paying certan debts of France to our citizens which will be from one to four millions; the western people may now estimate the value of their possessions. ————

I have been detained much longer than I expected but shall be with you by the last of this month. ————

Your sincere friend & Obt. Sert.

Meriwether Lewis.

Capt. Wm. Clark.

Note — write & direct to me at Cincinnatti.

2

THE TASK AHEAD

While Jefferson was getting approval from Congress, Lewis was busy with practical preparations. In March 1803 he went to the government arsenal at Harpers Ferry, Virginia (now West Virginia). Here he ordered such supplies as clothing, blankets, knapsacks, tools, and weapons. He also ordered 176 pounds of gunpowder, and rifles he himself had designed. He had the iron frame of a boat built, one that could be taken apart and packed for traveling. The craft was named the *Experiment*, and it took blacksmiths weeks to make it. In April he moved on to Lancaster, Pennsylvania, where he bought scientific equipment and studied celestial navigation. In May he was in Philadelphia, to buy maps, medical supplies, and presents for the Indians. These included handkerchiefs, scarlet cloth, assorted beads and brooches, tobacco, and shirts. He bought a few other provisions for which the expedition would be particularly grateful: material to make mosquito nets with; dried foodstuffs; waterproof gunpowder containers; and an air gun. The latter was not of much practical value, for it had little power or accuracy. But when the Indians found it could shoot without a loud noise or any smoke, they were very impressed.

So far, Jefferson and Lewis had been planning on a ten- or twelve-man expedition. Then Lewis decided that he needed a large, heavy boat. Thinking that the Indians upriver might be unfriendly, he ordered a fifty-five-foot vessel to be built at the Pittsburgh boatyards. This floating fortress would be capable of carrying ten tons—an impossible load for ten or twelve men to row up any river, especially the Missouri, which was famous for its swift currents.

Final page of a three-page letter from Lewis to Clark, August 3, 1803, five days after Lewis received Clark's acceptance of co-leadership of the expedition. In the next-to-last paragraph Lewis refers to the importance of the recently concluded Louisiana Purchase.

17

Meanwhile, Jefferson had prepared a list of written instructions for Lewis. The president wanted as much information as possible on the wildlife and climate of the regions the expedition would pass through, and he wanted these regions mapped and charted accurately. It was also important to learn about the Indian tribes they met and the chances for trade with them. Lewis was to invite Indian chiefs to visit the States and to offer an education to their children. He was also to teach them how to prevent smallpox epidemics. Having reached the Pacific, he was to see whether the fur-trade routes could be more efficiently organized. And, in case he died along the way, he was to name a member of the expedition to take over as leader.

Faced with such an immense task of exploration and research, Lewis decided he must share his command. He needed a fellow officer, a man he could trust. He thought of his friend William Clark, with whom he had served on the frontier.

William Clark had grown up much as Lewis had—with little formal education, but a great knowledge of the outdoors. His five brothers all took part in the American Revolution, but William, born in 1770, was too young for that war. When he was old enough, he joined the army and spent eight years on the frontier. In 1795 Lewis had joined Clark's rifle company, and a friendship developed between the two men. Then, in 1796, Clark returned to the family farm in Kentucky.

Lewis wrote to Clark and offered him a part in the expedition, with a rank equal to his own. Jefferson approved the choice. For although Lewis was known for his courage and adventurousness, it was possible that such qualities might lead him to take unnecessary risks. William Clark, four years older than Lewis, had a reputation as a solid and reliable soldier, trusted by whites and Indians alike. If the expedition found itself in danger, a calm, restraining hand might be necessary. Clark, in such a situation, would be able to rein in the more fiery Lewis.

Lewis was waiting in Pittsburgh for Clark's reply during the summer of 1803 and hurrying the boatbuilders to finish their work. Despite his growing impatience, the boat was not ready until the end of August. By then he had received Clark's enthusiastic reply, but one prob-

William Clark
(painting by Charles Wilson Peale)

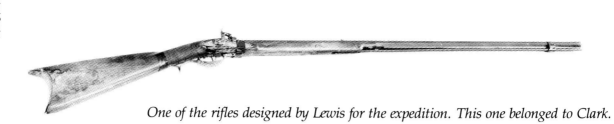

One of the rifles designed by Lewis for the expedition. This one belonged to Clark.

lem arose: The War Department did not give Clark the rank of captain for the expedition, as Lewis had requested. Instead Clark was given the rank of second lieutenant. Lewis was angry, and told Clark that no one should know of it. As far as the men on the expedition were concerned, they would both be captains.

Finally the boat was ready, and Lewis set off down the Ohio River with a few men, gathering more recruits on the way. Who were the men who made up the crew? In the journals kept by Lewis and Clark, only a few of them emerge as personalities. There was George Shannon, at eighteen the youngest man aboard. Shannon developed an annoying habit of getting lost in the middle of the wilderness and drifting back to camp days later, tired and hungry. And there was York, Clark's slave, who roused the curiosity of Indians who had never before seen a black man. John Colter was another. He later became famous as the first white man to see the hot springs of Yellowstone, a region that was nicknamed "Colter's Hell" in his honor. He also gained fame for an adventure with a group of hostile Blackfoot Indians who had captured him. They stripped him naked, gave him a headstart, then tried to run him down like an animal. Colter didn't even try to outrun them. Instead, he hid in a beaver lodge until they gave up the chase. Then he made his way over two hundred miles to the nearest fort.

Their most valued man, though, was George Drouilliard (pronounced "Drewyer," and spelled that way in the captains' journals). Drouilliard, a civilian, was an expert hunter, trapper, and scout, very tough and reliable, and he could communicate with Indians in sign language. Lewis and Clark soon came to depend heavily on Drouilliard.

In all, the members of the expedition numbered thirty, along with Lewis's Newfoundland dog, Scannon. They reached St. Louis in the fall, but as it was then too late in the year to set off up the Missouri, their departure was postponed until the spring.

In the months that followed, Lewis and Clark made plans, prepared their equipment, and began shaping their raw recruits into a tough, well-disciplined crew. All winter long they worked. At last the long-awaited day arrived. On May 14, 1804, the local citizenry turned out to see them off. The Lewis and Clark expedition was under way.

3

INTO THE FRONTIER

The men quickly settled into the routines of life on the river. The boat Lewis had had built in Pittsburgh was of the type called a "keelboat." Large as it was, it was not large enough to carry all these men plus the supplies and equipment needed for a journey of two years or more. So Lewis had bought two more boats, canoe-shaped craft called "pirogues," and he'd hired a band of French boatmen to crew them.

The easiest traveling came when a good breeze sprang up and a sail could be raised. Otherwise, when the bank was firm, the men jumped ashore and pulled the boats upstream by rope. But even the banks were not safe, for they often collapsed into the river. When this happened, there would be a muffled roar, and whole trees would be uprooted and go

Detail from a Mandan buffalo robe sent to Jefferson in 1805. The images depict the Mandan and their allies, the Minnetaree, in battle against the Sioux.

sailing down the river. This made the going even more dangerous.

Life wasn't made any easier by the insects during these early days. Mosquitoes, flies, ticks, and chiggers tormented the sweating men. The weather was hot, with violent thunderstorms that came up suddenly and threatened to swamp them. Men spent hours on end up to their waists in the swift river, and went for days without ever getting completely dry. Sore feet, boils, sunstroke, and rheumatism were common. Clark, a better boatman than Lewis, would stay with the men while Lewis explored the land they passed through. On these excursions Lewis collected many samples, and in the evening both men recounted the day's events in their journals.

By late June the expedition had reached the place where the river swings nearly due north—near the present-day site of Kansas City, Missouri. They had not as yet met any Indians, probably because the Indians were away hunting buffalo on the plains to the west. It would be another month before Drouilliard, while out hunting, found a Missouri Indian and brought him back to the river. The man told the captains that his people had lost so many of their number to disease that they'd joined up with the Oto Indians for safety. Sadly, it was the white fur traders and explorers who had brought the diseases that killed the Indians—smallpox, mainly, but even measles was deadly to these people.

While the Missouri went back to invite his people to meet the white men, the expedition moved on upriver. Three days later the meeting took place. The captains told the Oto chiefs that their land had passed from Spain to France to the United States. This must have sounded odd to

Clark's camp chest

the Indians, as they had no notion of the ownership of land. But they replied politely, and then passed the peace pipe around. Lewis and Clark distributed gifts, and a day later the expedition moved off again. But before it did, Lewis shot off his air gun. It caused a sensation among the Indians, who thought it magical.

This first meeting with Indians had ended in good feeling. Jefferson's message urging peace and cooperation between Indians and whites had been passed on. However, the explorers were not sure that the Sioux, whom they would meet next, would prove to be so friendly.

Before that meeting took place, one of the three sergeants, Charles Floyd, became seriously ill. Probably he was suffering from peritonitis, as a result of a ruptured appendix. The inflammation was fatal. Just before noon the next day Sergeant Floyd died. The expedition landed at a spot near present-day Sioux City, Iowa, and buried him on top of the highest hill in the area. This was to be the only death of an expedition member.

The Missouri River changes direction near Sioux City and swings to the northwest. It is here that the dense woods of the Midwest begin to thin out and the Great Plains begin. Soon the explorers started to notice more open country, with copses in low spots. On August 23 Joseph Fields killed the expedition's first buffalo. Lewis took eleven men out to help butcher the beast and bring in the carcass, which weighed between a thousand and fifteen hundred pounds.

On August 27 first contact was made

with the Sioux, and three days later a meeting was held beneath an oak tree across the river from what is today Yankton, South Dakota. The Sioux chiefs—these were Yankton Sioux—brought about seventy men and boys with them. Lewis made the usual speech, telling them that they were now subject to a new government. The Great Father—the president—would send men to trade with them. Then Lewis gave out presents—medals, clothes, and tobacco. The grand chief received a flag, a hat, and a coat richly decorated with lace. These Sioux were friendly, and one of the French boatmen, Old Dorion, stayed behind to help negotiate peace among the tribes. He also organized a group of chiefs who went to Washington to meet President Jefferson a couple of years later.

In early September an animal unknown to American science was sighted—the pronghorn antelope. In fact, these days were filled with discoveries of exotic

This 1908 painting by C. M. Russell depicts Western Indians' curiosity at their first sight of York, Clark's slave.

plant and animal life. There were herds of buffalo, of course, sometimes thousands strong. But by autumn the men were becoming cautious, for they were entering the territory of the Teton Sioux.

The Teton Sioux were a powerful, aggressive tribe, and their first meeting with Lewis and Clark occurred in late September. From the start there was tension and mistrust. These Indians did business with British traders from Canada, and didn't want the Americans to travel farther up the Missouri. During the days the expedition spent with them, there was the usual speech-making, giving of gifts, feasting, and smoking of the peace pipe. But there were several times when only the cool heads of the captains and a chief called Black Buffalo prevented open conflict.

One of these incidents occurred on the last night of the expedition's stay. After a feast in the Sioux village, two of the chiefs went back with the white men to spend the night on the keelboat. As the pirogue carrying them came in alongside the keelboat, the two craft collided, and the anchor cable of the keelboat snapped. The keelboat began to drift away, and in the confusion that followed the Indian chiefs thought they were being attacked. Within minutes the riverbank was crowded with armed warriors. The crew managed to get the boat under control, and the crisis passed. All the same, half the crew stood sentry all night. Clark, convinced that the Sioux intended to wipe out the expedition, did not sleep. When the expedition left the next morning, the men were relieved to have got past the Teton Sioux

without losing more than a few nights' rest.

Some good came of the adventure. Word traveled among the tribes that these white men were to be respected, that they stayed cool under pressure. When the expedition arrived among the Arikara Indians two weeks later, they were given a royal welcome.

The Arikara had a language entirely different from that of any of the Plains Indians Lewis and Clark had so far met. They were farmers rather than hunters, and they lived year round in earthen lodges. The Arikara were also merchants, and other tribes came hundreds of miles to trade for their crops of melon, corn, beans, squash, and tobacco. The Arikara had lost many of their number to smallpox, and also in battles with the Sioux.

It was just after they met the Arikara that the captains had a major discipline problem. One of the men, John Newman, was court-martialed for talking of mutiny. He received seventy-five lashes and was discharged from the expedition. He would leave the following spring with John Reed, a man who had tried to desert some weeks before. After the Newman incident, there were to be no major discipline problems.

By now, fall was turning to winter, and the crew began to find ice in puddles and frost on the ground. Clark was suffering badly from rheumatism but was still able

Painting, by Karl Bodmer, of a Minnetaree's "dog dance"

to keep up his journal accounts of meetings with the Indians along this stretch of the river. He mentions meeting the son of a chief who had recently died. The son had chopped off two of his own fingers, this being the tribal custom.

Finally, on October 24, 1804, the crew arrived at the place chosen for their winter quarters. They had traveled about sixteen hundred miles from St. Louis, and they were about sixty miles north of present-day Bismarck, North Dakota. They were among the Mandan Indians, but other tribes were also present, mainly the Minnetaree and the Amahami. These tribes had been decimated by smallpox, and had grouped together for protection against the Sioux.

Patrick Gass, a carpenter who had been promoted to sergeant after the death of Sergeant Floyd, supervised the building of a fort. It was made up of two rows of huts, joined at one point, with a palisade at the front facing the river. The men moved into the huts as they were completed. Fort Mandan was finally finished on Christmas Day. It flew the American flag, and was the westernmost military outpost of the United States.

It was during this time that Toussaint Charbonneau approached the captains and asked to be taken on as an interpreter. Charbonneau had been living with the Minnetaree for five years and spoke their language well. He had with him his wife, Sacagawea, a young Shoshoni girl who'd been captured by a Minnetaree war party far to the west.

The winter was a busy one in the Mandan villages. White traders and Assiniboin Indians came down from the north; Pawnee and Cheyenne came up from the

H. G. Hine's 1847 depiction of a buffalo hunt on the prairie

Sacagawea was to be valuable as a translator and in guiding the expedition through the Rockies, as depicted in this 1904 painting by Alfred Russell.

south; Arikara arrived from downriver. Eight or ten hunters went out every day for food for the expedition. As usual, the most valuable man around was George Drouilliard. He was almost never in the camp, as he led the hunters, and the party never once went hungry, thanks to him.

The captains energetically questioned everyone they met, gathering information on Indian languages and customs. Of course, they also learned what they could about the journey that lay ahead of them. Clark drew up a map based on the information they heard, and it was surprisingly accurate. They also learned about the grizzly bear, a beast they would soon encounter.

Captains Lewis and Clark also had more medical knowledge than anyone in the area, and they acted as physicians to the whole community. The treatment for most illnesses included "bleeding" the patient—making a cut and allowing the "bad blood" to flow out.

All winter long, Lewis and Clark prepared their reports and labeled their samples for President Jefferson, and on April 7, 1805, the keelboat set off downriver with the samples and a crew of six soldiers under the command of a corporal. Newman and Reed, the discharged men, went along. At the same time, the expedition set off upriver, intending to cross the Rocky Mountains before the next winter came.

4

A SECOND SPRING

The treeless plains stretched away to the horizon on all sides. On the riverbank grew cottonwood trees that shaded an undergrowth of wild roses and berry bushes. Flocks of geese and duck soared north along the flyway, and with every day the weather grew warmer. Sometimes the wind enabled the men to raise sails on the pirogues. More often it blew the wrong way, and made huge waves that almost swamped the boats.

On the fifth day out, disaster almost struck when the wind suddenly swung the white pirogue about. Toussaint Charbonneau was steering at the time. He panicked, and nearly capsized the boat. On board were all the expedition's instruments, papers, medicines, and the most valuable Indian presents. So were the two captains, three men who couldn't swim, and Sacagawea and her two-month-old

Painting by O. C. Seltzer of Lewis and Clark at Black Eagle Falls, on the Missouri River. Also pictured are York and, in the background, Sacagawea.

son, Jean-Baptiste. Drouilliard took the helm and righted the boat within seconds of disaster.

Later the same day they saw the enormous tracks of the bears the Mandan Indians had told them about. The Indians were very fearful of the fierce beasts, but the captains were not worried. They had confidence in their rifles.

Everything seemed big on the High Plains. The beaver in the river were fat and numerous, with thick fur. The buffalo herds were sometimes ten thousand strong. One day Clark watched a pack of wolves attacking a stray calf. He noticed that the cow defended her young only while the calf kept up with the herd. If it fell behind, the mother abandoned it to the wolves.

On April 26 they reached the junction of the Missouri and Yellowstone Rivers. Past this point, the low banks of the Missouri turned into high bluffs topped with sagebrush. It was around this time that Lewis, out hunting with another man, encountered his first grizzlies. The explorers shot the bears, and one of the two beasts ran away. But the other one, even though badly wounded, chased Lewis for eighty yards before the captain could reload his gun and finish off the beast. Six days later Clark and Drouilliard also came upon a huge bear. They put ten shots into it, five through the lungs, but the bear still had the strength to swim to a sandbar in the river. There it roared furiously for twenty minutes before dying. They stretched it out, and it measured 8 feet 7½ inches from nose to toe, 5 feet 10½ inches around the chest, and 3 feet 11 inches around the neck. They guessed its weight at around six hundred pounds.

The men also encountered less ferocious creatures. One was the bighorn sheep, which seemed to be able to go up and down the sides of cliffs with the

Filson Club, Louisville

Horn specimen from bighorn sheep, collected by the expedition in the Rockies and brought back on the return trip

greatest of ease. The hunters tried to shoot one, but the animal skipped away.

The landscape was becoming more hilly now, and the explorers knew they must be getting close to the Rockies. On May 26 Lewis climbed to the top of a hill and for the first time saw the Rocky Mountains in the distance. He was filled with awe at the sight of the snow-covered peaks glistening in the sunlight.

The traveling now became more difficult. The river was rapid and rocky, and the men had to tow the boats with ropes. The water was very cold, and sometimes the men would be in it up to their armpits for hours at a time. The rocks were sharp underfoot, and the men wore only moccasins. The ropes they used for towing were made of elkskin, and they often broke. When this happened, the boat would swing away, and there was always the chance it would swing into the rocks. Luckily, this never happened.

The weather was changing as well. The air of the open prairies had been dry and pure. Now the wind was accompanied by rainfall, often lasting all night. To make matters worse, the expedition had to keep clear of the cliffs that overlooked the river. Often, earth and stones would tumble down into the water beneath, sometimes from great heights.

But for all these difficulties, they did not complain. They had a well-deserved rest when, on June 2, the expedition arrived at a fork in the river. The waters of the northern branch were like the Missouri they knew, brown and muddy. The southern branch was clear and smooth and rapid. The captains reckoned that it must have flowed from the mountains. Knowing that the source of the Missouri was in the mountains, they took that branch to be the true Missouri. Just to be sure, Clark led a party down the southern branch, and Lewis took one up the northern. The character of the two streams did not change. Lewis named the northern branch after his cousin Maria, and to this day it is the Marias River.

The next problem was that the red pirogue would have to be left behind. What to do with all the gear it carried? A man called Pierre Cruzatte had the answer: Make a cache. This involved digging a round hole about two feet across and six or seven feet deep. The floor was covered with sticks, and the gear was piled on top. It was covered by skins; then the hole was filled in again with turf so that no one could tell anything had been buried. Cruzatte said that goods could be kept for years in a cache, as long as everything was dry. Then they tied the red pirogue to an island in the Marias to prevent its being swept away.

On June 11 they set off along the southern branch. Lewis went ahead, on foot, with four men. Clark and the others followed by boat. According to what the Indians had said, they must be nearing the Great Falls of the Missouri.

Sure enough, after three days Lewis and his party heard the sound of falling water and saw a great column of spray rising into the air. Lewis rushed down from the hill he'd been traveling along and saw a smooth sheet of water falling over a

Charles Wilson Peale's drawing of a preserved horned toad sent to Washington by the expedition

cliff at least eighty feet high. The next morning he sent a man back to Clark with the good news. The falls meant that they had taken the correct route.

Clark's party, meanwhile, was not doing so well. The men were in constant pain, for the river was full of sharp stones, on which they often cut their feet. Several of them were sick, and Sacagawea, who had fallen ill at the Marias fork, was now in critical condition. Clark had bled her, and done everything else he could think of. Nothing worked, and the young woman grew worse every day. Her husband, Charbonneau, did not help matters by insisting that the expedition turn around and go back to Fort Mandan.

But soon enough they joined up with Lewis's party at the head of the falls. Under Lewis's treatment, Sacagawea began to improve, much to Clark's relief. After several days of careful treatment the woman regained her health.

Now the men faced the problem of getting all their gear past the falls. Everything would have to be carried. This was a portage of eighteen miles, and Clark marked out the route with stakes. It was backbreaking work. The men built a couple of carts, but these kept breaking on the rough ground. The men were so tired that whenever they stopped to rest, they fell asleep. Frequent storms made the going much more difficult. At one point Clark, York, Sacagawea, little Baptiste, and Charbonneau took shelter from the rain and hail in a ravine. Moments later a great torrent of water came rushing down the ravine. They escaped just in time, and a number of things were lost, including the umbrella Clark had brought all the way from St. Louis.

The portage took four wretched days. When all the gear had finally been brought around, the expedition stayed put for a few days, to prepare for this next leg of the journey.

During this time Lewis assembled the *Experiment* and prepared to get it afloat. The only materials he could use to cover the frame of the boat were buffalo and elk hide. Hunters were sent out, and soon Lewis was stretching the hide over his

Engraving of the principal cascade of the Great Falls of the Missouri, possibly based on a sketch from Lewis's journal

boat. He then had the hides stitched together, but there was difficulty in sealing the holes properly, and the boat leaked badly. Disappointed, Lewis abandoned the boat he'd brought so far and had had such high hopes for. The men made a couple of dugout canoes from cottonwood trees instead.

On July 15 the new canoes were launched, and the party set off toward the mountains. They made good time now on the swift river. They passed abandoned Indian camps, fought clouds of mosquitoes, and were continually wet. Sacagawea was familiar with the plants they found, and could tell which were edible and what other uses they could be put to.

On July 18 they found a river they named the Dearborn, after the American secretary of war. They didn't realize it was one the Indians had told them about—a shortcut through the mountains to the Lolo Pass. The next day they reached a section of the river that seemed to cut between towering walls of black rock. There were very few places to step ashore, and the men had to row between these great rock walls, which Lewis called the "Gates of the Rocky Mountains."

Clark took a small party overland to look for Shoshoni, and after a week reached the point where the Missouri splits into three rivers, now called Three Forks. He left a note for Lewis there. Then he went on another twenty miles before returning to rejoin the expedition. No Shoshoni had been seen.

By the time the expedition was reunited at Three Forks, Clark had become very ill, so Lewis decided they would halt there. He sent scouting parties up the three rivers. These rivers were named the Jefferson, the Madison, and the Gallatin, after the president and his secretaries of state and the treasury. When the scouting parties came back, Lewis decided that the Jefferson was the correct river to follow, as the others headed too far south.

Though Clark usually acted as head scout, he was now too ill to explore farther up the Jefferson. So Lewis went out, with Drouilliard, Shields, and McNeal. One reason for their going ahead was that as the expedition hunted game, the rifle shots might alarm the Indians, but if a small scouting party could meet up with the Shoshoni first, that problem would be avoided. And it was now vital that they meet Shoshoni soon, and buy horses for the trek across the mountains.

Lewis and his three men found an Indian trail beside a stream and followed it past some high cliffs, which Lewis named Rattlesnake Bluffs. Then, on August 11, came the first sighting of a Shoshoni—the one whom Shields had scared away. Contact was made a couple of days later, however, and Lewis persuaded the Indians to return with him to meet Clark and the rest of the expedition. The Shoshoni were very nervous, fearing a trap. Lewis could only hope, as they approached the rendezvous, that Clark and the others had made it. But as he drew near, accompanied by the Shoshoni, he realized that Clark had not arrived. At that moment, Lewis knew the whole expedition was at stake.

Food in the wilderness

What did the members of the expedition eat as they worked their way across the wilderness? For the most part, they hunted for their food, but they also carried with them staples that would not go bad: bags of grain, sugar, beans, and peas; barrels of flour, salt, and salt pork. In the early days, when the party was close to civilization and game was scarce, they ate from this larder. Hominy, or grits, was a common breakfast, with pork at midday and supper.

After about a month, however, game became more plentiful. The hunters would ride ahead of the expedition and hang what they shot from a tree—out of reach of the wolves but where it could be seen from the boats. The best pieces were eaten first, the hams and tenderloins of the deer, the hump and the tongue of the buffalo. Nothing was wasted. Bones were cracked for their marrow, and hides were converted to moccasins or clothing. The fat would be used for candles, soap, soup stock, and insect repellent.

Deer, elk, antelope, and buffalo were all plentiful until the expedition reached the foothills of the Rockies. Often the hunters would end up with a surplus of big game, and the meat they couldn't eat was dried for later use.

Their favorite game proved to be the fat Missouri beaver, particularly its liver and tail. A good-size beaver made a meal for two men, and George Drouilliard, the expedition's best hunter, excelled at trapping them.

The men didn't eat only meat. They found cress and kale growing wild, and fresh fruit was very plentiful during the summer. After Sacagawea joined the expedition at Fort Mandan, she added variety to the diet by collecting and preparing edible plants such as prairie turnips and wild onions.

But there were to be hard times after the expedition left the Great Plains. Close to starvation in the Rockies, they reluctantly ate horse meat for the first time. Curiously, they grew to like it. The same was true of dog meat, which all the men except Captain Clark became very fond of. Lewis wrote that while they were forced to live on dog meat they were stronger and healthier than at any other time during the trip.

Across the Rockies they had their first taste of salmon, which Clark considered the finest fish he ever tasted. But the salmon run was ending when they reached the Columbia, and their Pacific winter was not a happy one from the point of view of diet. The dried fish and meat that they had with them went bad in the damp air, and the elk they hunted were lean and stringy.

The members of the expedition came to like some of the new fare they partook of in the wilderness, but as they approached St. Louis at the end of the journey, they all cheered loudly at the sight of the first cow.

When Lewis and his party had left Clark at Three Forks, they had spent a day traveling up the valley of the Jefferson. Then that river forked, too. Lewis had left behind a note, mounted on a stick, telling Clark to wait there till he returned. The water here was so shallow that the canoes would be able to go no farther. It was to this meeting place that Lewis now led the Shoshoni, expecting the canoes to have come up this far.

Lewis was a quick thinker. First he gave the chief his gun, telling him that if there was trickery, the chief could shoot him. Then he sent Drouilliard to get the note that Lewis himself had left on the stick for Clark. Lewis pretended that the note—which of course the chief couldn't read—was from Clark. He pretended that it said that Clark was still coming up the river, and that Lewis should wait here for him. He suggested to the chief that Drouilliard and a few of the Shoshoni go down to meet Clark the next day while he and the other two white men stay with the chief. The Indians were very suspicious. Lewis knew that if they gave up on him now, they'd go into the mountains and there would be no horses.

The chief trusted him, and they all settled down for the night. Some of the Shoshoni hid themselves in the undergrowth, fearing an attack. As for Lewis, he slept very little. He knew that the expedition now depended on the trust of the Shoshoni chief. And that could vanish in a moment.

The next morning, the chief was still with them. Drouilliard set off with a few

Indians and eventually found Clark and the rest of the expedition coming up the river. When Sacagawea saw the Shoshoni with Drouilliard, she became very excited. She indicated that these were her own people. It was a very happy meeting, and the Shoshoni were singing as they escorted Clark and his group to Lewis and the chief.

Sacagawea now had a very emotional time as she was reunited with old childhood friends. The most dramatic incident occurred when Lewis and Clark sat down for a meeting with the chief, whose name was Cameahwait. Sacagawea was there to help translate. Suddenly she leapt up, rushed to the chief, and threw her arms around him: Cameahwait was her brother.

The captains learned that the Shoshoni were a very poor tribe, that they had to keep to the mountains for fear of their enemies, the Blackfoot Indians. But in the fall they joined up with their allies, the Flathead, and other tribes, and felt brave enough to come down to the plains to hunt buffalo.

But the chief also told them that it was not possible to get through the mountains by following the Salmon River, a large stream about eighteen miles from the Shoshoni village. It flowed between cliffs so high that neither people nor horses could cross them. It was possible, though, to cross by a mountain pass some distance to the north.

By the time Clark got back from a scouting trip along the Salmon River, Lewis had bought about thirty horses

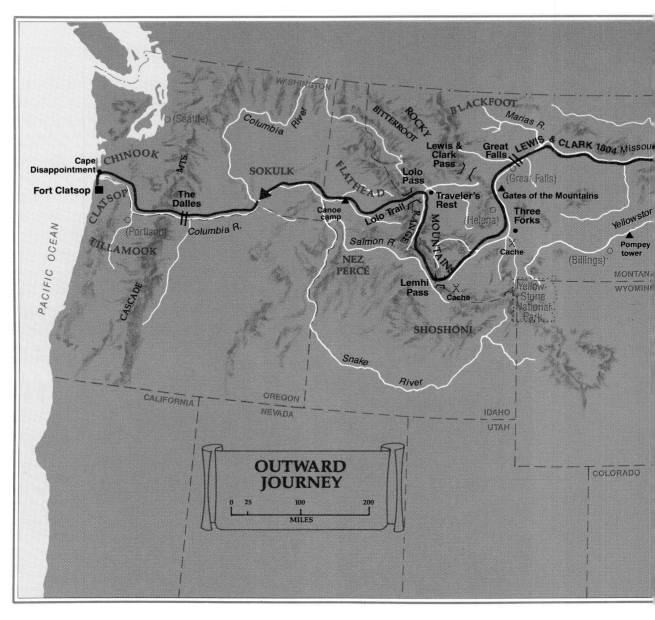

Map labels:
WASHINGTON · (Seattle) · Columbia River · BITTERROOT · ROCKY · BLACKFOOT · Marias R. · LEWIS & CLARK 1804 Missouri · CHINOOK · Cape Disappointment · Lewis & Clark Pass · Great Falls · Fort Clatsop · SOKULK · FLATHEAD · Lolo Pass · (Great Falls) · The Dalles · Canoe camp · Traveler's Rest · Gates of the Mountains · CLATSOP · (Portland) · Columbia R. · Lolo Trail · (Helena) · Three Forks · Yellowstone · PACIFIC OCEAN · TILLAMOOK · Salmon R. · RANGE · MOUNTAINS · Cache · (Billings) · Pompey tower · NEZ PERCÉ · Lemhi Pass · Cache · Yellow-Stone National Park · MONTANA · WYOMING · CASCADE · SHOSHONI · Snake · River · Yellowstone National Park · CALIFORNIA · OREGON · IDAHO · NEVADA · UTAH · COLORADO

OUTWARD JOURNEY

0 25 100 200
MILES

from the Shoshoni. The next day the expedition set off, after saying good-bye to these friendly Indians. Buying the horses had not been easy, for the Shoshoni needed them for the buffalo hunt they were about to make. Lewis was forced to exchange guns for the horses.

There followed a long, hard, and dangerous journey through the Bitterroot Mountains, broken only by a friendly meeting with Flathead Indians. It rained and snowed, and the westward stretch over the Lolo Trail was particularly difficult. The hillsides were steep, and there was no game to be had. When their stocks of food ran out, they were forced to eat their colts. Clark took a small group of hunters on ahead. The others trailed be-

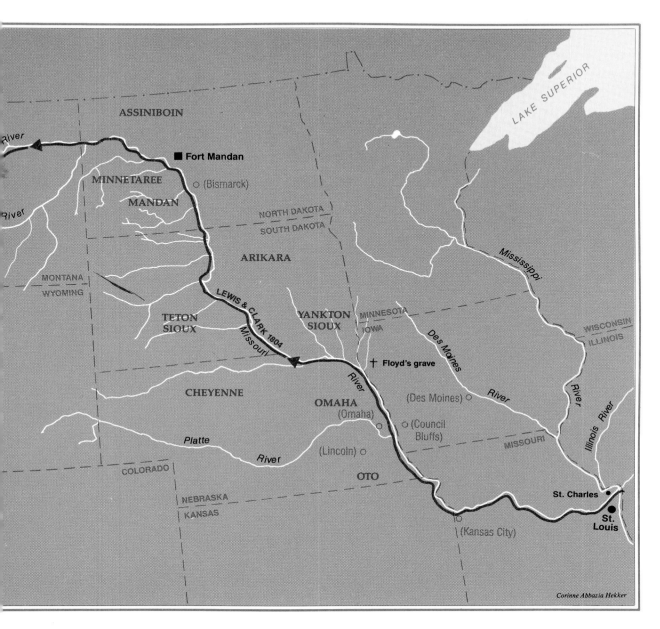

Corinne Abbazia Hekker

hind, growing feebler and colder every day.

All Clark's group managed to kill was a stray horse. They ate some for breakfast and hung the rest on a tree for the men who followed. Two days later they finally came through the mountains, to their great relief, and found an Indian village of the Nez Percé (French for "pierced nose").

These Indians gave Clark and his men dried salmon and camas root, which made them all sick, for they were not used to such food. Clark learned from the Nez Percé that they were on the Clearwater River, only seven days' journey from the Columbia. The Columbia, as they knew, flowed into the Pacific.

Two days later Lewis and the rest of

37

C. M. Russell's 1905 painting depicts the expedition's encounter with the Flathead Indians. At the right, Clark and Lewis observe as an Indian guide interprets for them. Sacagawea sits nearby while York tends the horses.

the expedition arrived. Lewis's men were promptly sick, as Clark's had been, after eating the strange food of the Nez Percé. As they recovered, Clark set them to making dugout canoes, and in two weeks they had made five.

On October 7 they left the Nez Percé village in the dugouts. They passed through some of the strangest and most awesome land they had yet seen, but in their haste to get to the sea they paid it little attention. They paddled from the Clearwater into the Snake River, at what today is the Idaho-Washington border, and six days later they entered the Columbia, where they were warmly welcomed by the Sokulk Indians.

The expedition camped here, and stocked up on food. The salmon run was over by this time of the year, so the captains bought forty dogs from the friendly

Sokulk. They paid for them with bells, beads, and thimbles.

Soon they were on their way again. For the next three weeks they raced toward the ocean through fast-flowing waters. They had to make one portage at the Celilo Falls, but when they reached a very turbulent stretch of rapids known as the Dalles, no portage was possible. To the amazement of the onlooking Indians, they took the canoes through the rapids and emerged safe and sound. With winter so close, the captains were prepared to take chances they normally would have avoided.

Early in November the Cascade Mountains were passed, and on the 7th they at last sighted the ocean. Pacific means "peaceful," but Clark did not think it a peaceful ocean. The sea roared, the rain never stopped, and the wind blew with great violence. The men were very miserable, for though they were so close to the ocean, they still had a few difficult miles to go. The river was six miles broad at its estuary, and very rough, causing seasickness.

Clothing now became a serious problem, for all their buckskin was soaked and rotting. Clark realized that if they were not able to shoot game before winter and use the hides for making new garments, they would be in trouble. The Chinook Indians were also a problem on the lower Columbia. These Indians had for years been brutally treated by fur traders, and they were given to stealing the expedition's property.

It became vital that the expedition find a place to spend the winter. The site finally chosen was on the south side of the

The expedition met the Chinook Indians on the lower Columbia in November 1805. In this 1905 painting by C. M. Russell, Sacagawea can be seen at right, speaking to the Chinook in sign language.

river, where elk were to be found. Elk were needed not only for their meat but also for their hides, to replace the expedition's rotten buckskin clothing.

By Christmas Day the men had finished building their fort, which they named Fort Clatsop after a local tribe, and had moved into their cabins. Life was not very pleasant, however. It rained constantly, all the whiskey was gone, and the meat and fish spoiled quickly in the damp air.

What the men needed most at this stage was salt. Salt would cover the taste of the bad meat. A group were sent to the seashore, and there they spent days boiling seawater in huge kettles until the insides of the kettles were coated with salt. This was then scraped into a barrel.

A trip to the coast to see a beached

During the winter at Fort Clatsop, Clark made this map of Celilo Falls, on the Columbia River, showing the portage around the falls.

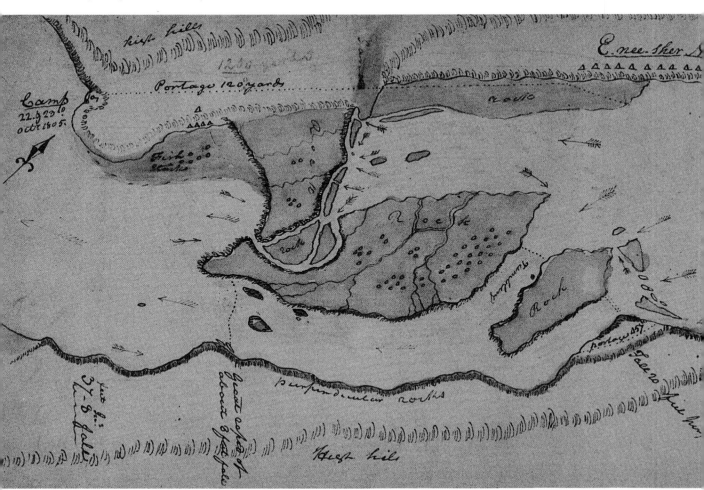

whale proved to be the highlight of a dreary winter. Drouilliard soon began to find more elk, but the meat was poor and thin at this time of year. The men made new clothes from the hides, and the salt makers kept busy at the seashore.

Lewis and Clark worked over their journals. The trip from Fort Mandan to the coast was over territory that no scientist had yet studied, and the captains also made sketches of everything from tools to fish, from Indian dress to canoe designs. This documenting of the journey west would be the captains' most crucial task during the bitter winter.

5

HOMEWARD

On March 23, 1806, the expedition set off on the homeward journey. Going up the Columbia, they met many of the same tribes they had met coming downriver the previous fall. It was difficult to buy food, however. Provisions were low and prices were high. On April 9 they came again to the rapids and had to use a tow rope to pull their canoes through. Soon after this they were able to buy horses, although at a very high price.

On they went. They left the Celilo Falls and the treacherous rapids behind, and followed the Columbia on horseback until it turned north. Then they cut across country due east. Soon the Nez Percé came out to greet them and were as friendly as they had been the previous winter. But still food was a problem. The Indians had only roots, and the explorers

Junction of the Yellowstone and Missouri Rivers, where Clark's party and Lewis's reunited after having split up at Traveler's Rest (painting by Karl Bodmer)

had no food at all. They sold the buttons off their coats for something to eat. Clark even sold his medical services for food. They spent some time among the Nez Percé, waiting for the snow to melt in the high passes. The captains organized a council with a number of Nez Percé chiefs and expressed their government's wish for peaceful trading relations with the Indians. As usual, the translation process was tedious, and the council took almost the whole day.

By now the party was camped on the banks of the Clearwater River. The hunting was better here, and Lewis watched the river every day for signs of floodwater from the melted snows of the high mountain passes. The men were now impatient to cross the Rockies and get back to the plains, where the buffalo grazed. On June 10 they set out over the Bitterroot Mountains. They had no guides, for the Nez Percé were afraid of meeting their enemies, the Blackfoot and the Minnetaree. Once in the high mountains, the party

Clark's map of the mouth of the Columbia River. At lower right is the site of the temporary encampment of November 16–25. The expedition then moved to the south bank of the river and began to construct Fort Clatsop.

found the snow still twelve to fifteen feet deep, and they had to turn back.

When they next tried to cross, they had Indian guides with them. On June 29 they crossed the Lolo Pass and got through the Bitterroots. Soon game was again plentiful, and the party rested, greatly relieved to have the Rockies finally behind them.

On the way out, the expedition had made a big U from the Great Falls of the

Missouri down through the Gates of the Mountains, west across the Lemhi Pass, and up through the Bitterroots to the Lolo Trail. Now it was decided that Lewis should take a party straight across the open top of that U shape. That party would then explore the Marias River area. Clark and the rest of the expedition would follow the original route to Three Forks. There they would retrieve the boats left in the fall. Then Sergeant Ordway would take a canoe party down the Missouri to meet up with Lewis at the Great Falls. Together they would travel on down the Missouri. Clark's group would meanwhile come down the unexplored Yellowstone River, and meet the others at the junction of the Yellowstone and the Missouri. In their instructions from the president, the captains were asked to find the sources of rivers that flowed into the Missouri. They were particularly curious to see if the Marias opened up the Canadian country, with its rich fur harvest.

The more dangerous trip was Lewis's, as his party was going deep into Blackfoot country. By July 25, after three weeks, he had had enough and was ready to return to the Missouri, disappointed to find that the Marias curved westward, rather than north. In the following days the group almost ended their journey in those bleak plains of northern Montana. They met a group of Blackfoot Indians, and after smoking a pipe with them, Lewis agreed to camp with them by the river. The captain was mistrustful of the Indians, and kept a careful watch all night. But the next morning two of the men were careless, and the Indians managed to seize their guns. The two men, Joseph and Reuben Fields, went after the thieves. They caught up with them, and there was a struggle. Then one of the Indians fell dead, stabbed through the heart by Reuben Fields.

Meanwhile, Lewis and Drouilliard were fighting for their guns, which the other Indians were trying to take. Having got the guns back, they then had to prevent the Indians from taking their horses. Lewis dashed after them as they drove the horses into a ravine. He shouted that he would shoot unless they gave him his horse. One of the Indians turned, and Lewis shot him through the belly. The Indian fell, mortally wounded, and fired back, narrowly missing Lewis. The other Indians fled, leaving half their horses and nearly all their weapons behind.

The explorers then left in a great hurry. They covered more than a hundred miles over very rough ground in the course of one day. The next day, the men were weary, but Lewis urged them on. He wanted to get as far away from Blackfoot country as possible, for the Indians knew he was to meet the rest of the expedition at the river, and Lewis feared they would ambush the others before he could get there and warn them. Finally, they reached the river. There they saw the expedition's canoes coming downstream. They happily let the horses go and climbed into the canoes.

They drifted downriver for several days toward the place where they were to meet Clark. For a change, life was easy. There was game to be had, and the weather was pleasant. At the meeting place—the junction of the Yellowstone and the Missouri—they found a note from Clark saying he had gone on downstream, so they followed.

Clark's trip had gone well. His group— twenty men, Sacagawea and the baby, and fifty horses—crossed the mountains over a trail easier than the one used in the winter. This was later called Gibbon's Pass. They reached the forks of the Jefferson on July 8, and found the canoes and other supplies they had cached there the previous year. The trip downriver was a fast one. At Three Forks, Sergeant Ordway and a small group took the canoes

Assiniboin woman's dress, of mooseskin and beadwork, brought east by Lewis and Clark in 1806

Peabody Museum, Harvard University

45

and most of the baggage on downstream, later to meet Lewis and his party at the end of their great ride. Clark and the rest set off by land for the Yellowstone River. The only problem was with the horses. The stony ground wore their hooves down, so Clark made coverings for them of tanned buffalo hide.

One night, they had half their horses stolen by Indians, but by that time they'd almost finished making a pair of dugout canoes. Sergeant Pryor and three men were sent ahead to Fort Mandan with the horses while the rest came on by river. On July 25 they stopped to look at a great tower of rock that rose two hundred feet above the flat plains. Clark carved his name and the date on the rock face, where it can still be seen. He named the tower after Sacagawea's baby—Pompey's Pillar.

Soon they were seeing buffalo again, and the fat beaver with the rich pelts. But by August 3, when they reached the Missouri, the mosquitoes had become unbearable. They left a note for Lewis at the meeting place and carried on downstream. Even so, the insects were very bad, and sleep was impossible.

Sergeant Pryor came drifting downstream on August 8. Indians had stolen his horses, so he and his men had come on foot until they'd shot a couple of buffalo. They made two little "bull boats," like those used by the Mandan. These were basin-shaped craft made of a framework of saplings with buffalo hide stretched over them.

On August 12 the expedition was reunited, and two days later they reached the Mandan villages. Here the two cap-

tains attempted to mend the breach that had opened between the Mandan and the Arikara. They also tried to persuade some of the chiefs to come to Washington with them. Only one agreed, a Mandan chief named Sheheke, or "Big White."

John Colter came to the captains then and asked to be discharged. He had no wish to return to civilization, he said, and the captains agreed to let him go his own way. Toussaint Charbonneau was also discharged, there being little need at this point for an interpreter. Sacagawea went with him, and Clark was sad to see them go. He offered to bring up little Baptiste,

Portrait of a Mandan chief by George Catlin, 1832

The language barrier

For many years before Lewis and Clark began their historic trip, Frenchmen had been hunting, trapping, and trading in the Louisiana Territory. Many of these men had actually settled in Indian villages, and most of them had learned the languages of the Indians they traded with. For this reason the captains were able to communicate with the tribes they met on the Missouri.

Lewis, Clark, and Sacagawea

Sometimes one of the French boatmen would do the interpreting, sometimes a French trader who happened to be living with the tribe. It was Pierre Cruzatte, a boat-man, who acted as interpreter when Lewis and Clark met the Teton Sioux. Cruzatte found the language diffi-cult, and Lewis had to cut his speech short. But the Teton Sioux had prisoners from the Omaha tribe, and this language Cruzatte knew better. He discovered from the Omaha that the Teton did not intend to let the expedition proceed. This information was valuable in putting the Americans on their guard.

It was when they met the Shoshoni that the process became truly complex. Cameah-wait, the Shoshoni chief, would speak to Sacagawea, who would then translate into Minnetaree for her husband. Charbonneau would then translate from Minnetaree into French, but not into English. It took Francis Labiche, another Frenchman, to translate the message from French into English. Then the captains would reply, and their words would go back the same way—English into French, French into Minnetaree, then Minne-taree into Shoshoni.

This was still not the worst of it. When they met the Flathead Indians, the chain was increased by one link, for Sacagawea would speak in Shoshoni to a small boy of the Flathead tribe, and he would then translate the message into his own tongue for the chiefs. With so many possibilities for misunderstanding, it's a wonder the Americans got on as well as they did with the various tribes they met.

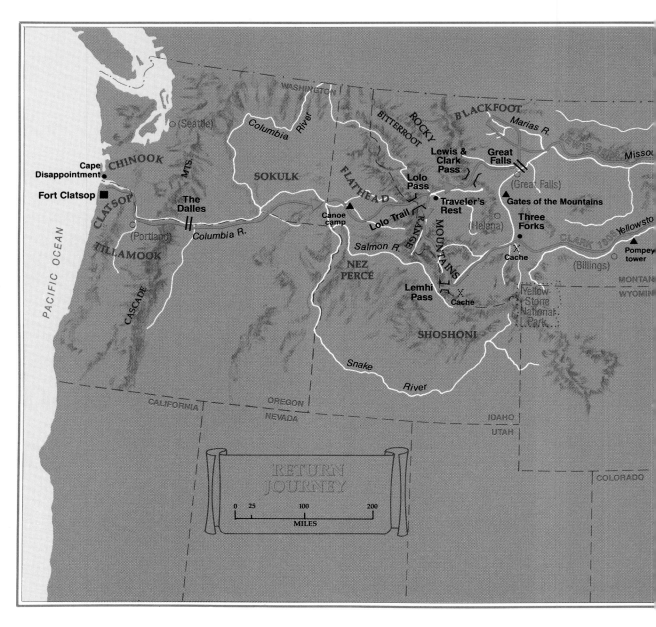

but Sacagawea said he was still too young to leave his mother. Later, though, the little boy would come to Clark.

They left the Mandan villages on August 17 and traveled downstream. They reached the first Arikara village four days later. Sheheke, the Mandan chief, met the Arikara chiefs, and they agreed to make peace. On the 30th they passed some Teton Sioux, but Clark would not stop. He berated them for their bad behavior of two years before, and the expedition moved on.

They were moving quickly now, covering sixty to eighty miles each day. They met traders and trappers going upstream, and were given hearty welcomes and generous provisions. On September 20 the

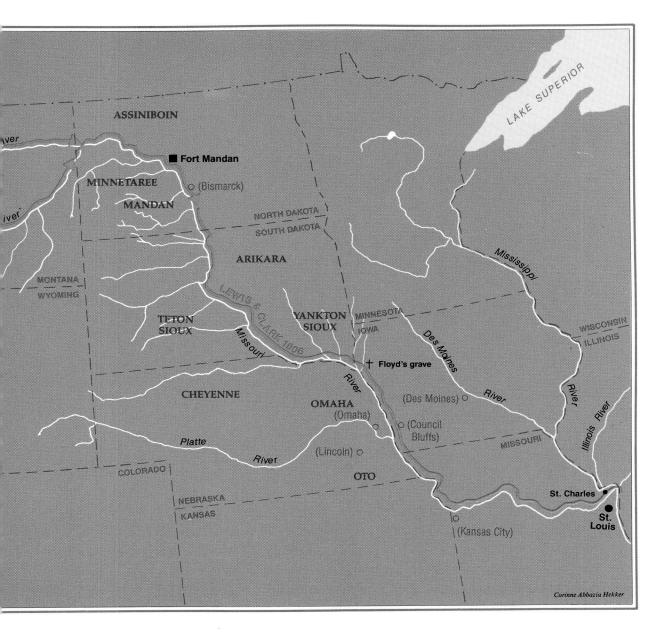

Corinne Abbazia Hekker

men cheered when they saw cows on the bank. They stayed that night at a French settlement, and the next day at the village of St. Charles. They were told that they had been given up for lost. One rumor had it that they had been gobbled up by wild animals; another, that they had been wiped out by Indians; a third, that they had been enslaved by Spaniards. There was great rejoicing, and then they carried on down to St. Louis.

The whole town turned out, on September 23, 1806, to welcome home the buckskin-clad explorers. The adventure had lasted two years and four months and covered 7,500 miles. The first men to cross the North American continent were home again.

AFTERWORD

NEW FRONTIERS

By the end of the winter that the expedition spent by the Pacific, Clark had finished his map of the territory from Fort Mandan to Fort Clatsop. It showed that no practical all-water route across the continent existed. This had been an old dream. Thomas Jefferson, among others, had imagined a trade route being opened that would connect the headwaters of the Missouri to the headwaters of the Columbia. But Clark's map, the first accurate one to be made of the region, told the sad truth: There was no easy trade route from the Atlantic to the Pacific.

This, then, was one accomplishment—the discovery that no all-water route to the Pacific existed. But the route that Lewis and Clark did find was feasible for travel, and in 1811 the agents of John Jacob Astor used it to cross the continent. They set up a fur-trading post called Astoria, at the

*William Clark in 1832
(painting by George Catlin)*

mouth of the Columbia. It made Astor America's first millionaire.

Later explorers and emigrants found easier ways of reaching the Pacific. The Oregon Trail went directly across the plains and over the mountains to the south of the Lewis and Clark route, and other more southerly routes were discovered. Still, Lewis and Clark were the first to show that it was possible. This is a second achievement: The expedition opened up the frontier, threw light on what had before been largely unknown, and inspired others to follow. As Jefferson had hoped, hunters, trappers and settlers were soon moving up the river and spreading out over the plains. Later still came the wagon trains, bringing farmers and their families to the West.

All this settlement helped establish the U.S. claim to the Oregon country, and by 1870 the borders of the United States were what they are today. For this Lewis and Clark may take credit: They helped

Clark's journal inside its hide binding

turn the U.S. from a coastal to a continental nation.

Lewis and Clark's scientific discoveries were also impressive. They discovered 24 Indian tribes, and 178 plants and 122 animals then unknown to North American science. These included the pronghorn antelope, the bull snake, the tern, the prairie dog, the jackrabbit, the grouse, the pelican, the porcupine, and the coyote. They even found the spine of what they thought had been a huge fish, and took along a few bones for Jefferson. In fact, the bones belonged not to a fish but to a prehistoric reptile.

This was all in accordance with Jefferson's instructions. The reports that Lewis and Clark prepared for him were different from the reports of other explorers, who usually just looked for the best way to make quick profits. Lewis and Clark had the fur trade in mind and made many suggestions as to how the United States could get the better of the British. They also described in detail the customs and languages of the Indian tribes they had met. From Fort Mandan they had sent Jefferson several boxes and a large trunk full of horns, skins, and skeletons, and three cages containing live creatures.

Clark's journal entry for February 16, 1806, included this sketch of a buzzard's head along with descriptions of the species, its manner of flight, and other details.

are 4¾ inches   in length and of
a whitish   colour uncovered
with feathers,   they are not
entirely   smooth but
not imbricated;   the toes are four
in number three   of which are
forward and that   in the center

much the longest; the fourth is short and is inserted
near the inner of the three other toes and rather pro-
jecting forward. the thye is covered with feathers
as low as the Knee. the top or upper part of the toes
are imbricated with broad scales lying transversly,
the nails are black and in proportion to the size of
the bird comparitively with those of the Hawk or
Eagle, short and bluntly pointed. the under
side of the wing is covered with white down and
feathers. a white stripe of about 2 inches in
wedth, also marks the outer part of the wing, in-
=bracing the lower points of the feathers, which
over the joints of the wing through their whole
length or wedth of that part of the wing. all
the other feathers of whatever part are of a glossy
shineing black except the down, which is not
glossy, but equally black. the skin of the beak
and head to the joining of the neck is of a pale
orrange Yellow, the other part uncovered with
feathers is of a light flesh colour. the skin is
thin and wrinkled except on the beak where it
is smooth.   this bird fly's very clumsily. nor
do I know whether it ever seizes its prey alive, but

There was a prairie dog in one, a sharp-tailed grouse in another, and four magpies in the third. There were Indian artifacts—bows and arrows, pottery, clothing, buffalo robes—all carefully labeled.

Jefferson had also wanted Lewis and Clark to establish friendly relations with the Indian tribes they met. In this the explorers were successful, for the most part, but the friendships between Indian and white man did not last. They began to collapse as more and more hunters, trappers and settlers moved in on the Indians'

hereditary lands. At the same time, Indian populations were being devastated by such "new" diseases as smallpox and alcoholism. So the opening up of the West was a mixed blessing. For the Indians, it did vastly more harm than good.

And what became of the brave men—and woman—of the expedition? Some dropped completely out of sight. Others accepted 320-acre plots of land west of the Mississippi. Congress had granted these bonuses in 1807, plus double pay, to all the men. Several reenlisted in the army. John Colter, who left the expedition at the Mandan villages, retired a few years later to La Charrette, where he had a farm near Daniel Boone's. He married an Indian woman, and died after only three years of retirement in 1813.

George Drouilliard went back to the Rockies. He was killed by Blackfoot Indians near Three Forks in 1810. As for George Shannon, the youngest of the group, who had been lost three times during the expedition, he had an exciting future. He want back up the Missouri in 1807 with some of the other men of the expedition. This party was attacked by Sioux, angry over the loss of one of their chiefs who had gone to Washington and died there. Four white men were killed and nine injured. Shannon was shot in the leg, which had to be amputated, but he recovered. In 1810 he helped with the publication of the captains' journals. He became a lawyer and a state senator of Missouri, and died in 1838.

Sacagawea probably died in 1812, leaving not only Jean-Baptiste but a little girl

Missouri Historical Society

Clark's drawing and description of this coastal fish was entered into his journal on February 25, 1806.

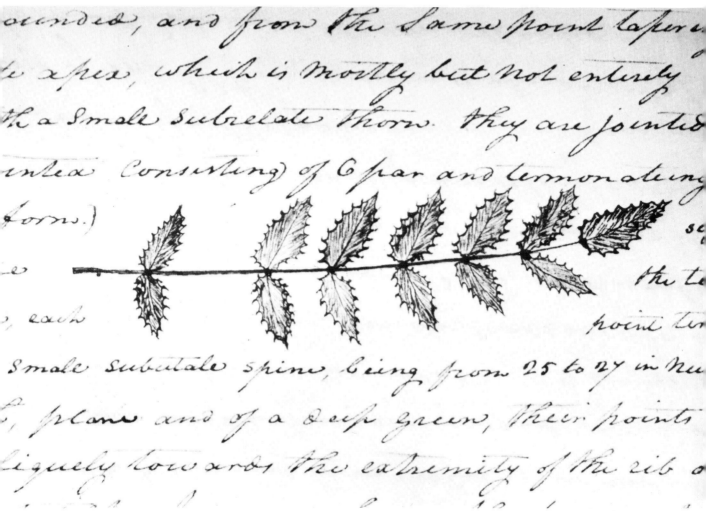

Evergreen drawing from Clark's journal, April 10, 1806

called Lizette. But it's difficult to be sure of Sacagawea's fate. In 1884 an old woman called Sacagawea died among the Shoshoni. She had known many details of the expedition, and it's possible that this was the woman who had helped Lewis and Clark get through the mountains.

Sacagawea remains one of the most celebrated women in American history. It's not hard to see why. First of all, she carried a tiny infant with her on that long, hard journey from Fort Mandan to the coast. This didn't prevent her from being one of the most valuable members of the expedition. She was able to show the men which plants were edible when there was no game to be had, and when the expedition finally made contact with the Shoshoni, her own people, it was largely thanks to her that these wary Indians

Tribes along the way

Lewis and Clark reported to Jefferson on more than a hundred Indian tribes. The expedition had direct dealings with only half a dozen or so, however. Of these, the first were the Oto and the Missouri, Indian nations greatly reduced in numbers by smallpox. The meeting occurred at what is today Council Bluffs, Iowa, and there was much speech-making and giving of gifts. Basically, Lewis told the Indians that they were now under a new government, and that the Great Father (the president) wanted peaceful trading relations. In return he would give them protection.

This meeting went fairly smoothly, as did the next, a month later, with the Yankton Sioux. These Indians lived in large, conical lodges made of poles covered with buffalo skins painted red and white, and wore buffalo robes and leggings. The Yankton Sioux wore body paint and ornamented themselves with bear claws, feathers, and porcupine quills. Lewis and Clark were impressed by the "dignity and boldness" of the Yankton Sioux, who agreed to send representatives to Washington the next year.

Things did not go so well with the Teton Sioux. These Indians shaved their heads, apart from a center strip, and the hair from this strip was braided behind. From the head of the main chief hung a long string of eagle feathers. Between the Teton Sioux and the white men there was a good deal of tension, and on several occasions there was almost bloodshed. Still, they smoked the red-clay peace pipe together in front of a lodge of buffalo skins big enough to hold seventy people.

The expedition wintered at Fort Mandan among three loosely joined tribes—the Mandan, Minnetaree, and Amahami—about 4,400 in number. There were five villages, each surrounded by sturdy earthen walls behind which moundlike lodges clustered, each lodge large enough for several families, their horses, and their dogs. It was here that Clark wrote his preliminary report on the Indian tribes of the Missouri.

The first sign of the Shoshoni—the next tribe they would meet—came in the foothills of the Rockies: a huge lodge about fifty feet high and seventy feet across. The Shoshoni lived in the mountains but came down to hunt buffalo in the fall. They were very poor, and close to starving when Lewis met them. But they did have horses in abundance, and it was horses that the expedition needed at this stage. Thanks largely to Sacagawea, the Shoshoni provided the expedition with its transportation over the Rockies.

The expedition met the Flathead Indians in a valley in the mountains. These were described as stout, light-skinned people who spoke very strangely, with a sort of gurgling sound. They were friendly to the party, as were the Nez Percé, who lived on the western slopes of the Rockies.

From there the party traveled quickly down the Clearwater River to the Snake and Columbia Rivers, meeting the Sokulk, Chinook, Clatsop, and Tillamook tribes. These coastal tribes all had big, well-designed canoes, which they handled very expertly. The Chinook were remarkable in that they compressed and reshaped their infants' heads by means of boards, as shown in the sketches from Clark's journal, below. Clark's notes here

refer to "Flat head Indians," but the tribe known as the Flathead, farther east up the Columbia, did not practice "head flattening"; rather, they were named the Flathead by the coastal tribes, who considered the tops of their neighbors heads to be flat.

On their way back the expedition met the same tribes again, naturally, with one exception—the Blackfoot, whom Lewis and his party met up the Marias River. These were the Indians who tried to steal the crew's horses and guns. The two Indians killed in the ensuing struggle were the only Indian casualties suffered at the hands of the expedition.

Among specimens collected and described by the captains, and later illustrated by ornithologists, were "Clark's crow" (center) and "Lewis's woodpecker" (right).

were persuaded to sell the horses that the white men so desperately needed.

Lewis and Clark owed a great deal to this brave and capable woman. Captain Clark repaid this debt when he took over the education of Sacagawea's children, plus that of another Charbonneau child, by a different wife, this one a boy with his father's name, Toussaint. Jean-Baptiste grew up under Clark's guidance, and as a young man he had the good fortune to travel to Europe, where he studied Latin, German, literature, and philosophy. He returned to the West and became a famous mountain man and guide. He died among the Shoshoni at the age of sixty-one. Toussaint Charbonneau, Sr., lived among the Indians for the rest of his life and died in 1840, at the age of eighty.

As for the leaders of the expedition, Clark was offered 1,000 acres by Congress, and Lewis 1,600. Lewis refused, because he had promised Clark that their rewards would be equal. So Congress gave them each 1,600 acres. Clark had a steady, happy life, and died in 1838, at age sixty-eight. He served as superintendent of Indian Affairs for many years, and was liked and trusted by the Indians. He was the first governor of the Missouri Territory, and was reappointed three times. He married Julie Hancock shortly after his return from the Pacific, and they had five children. He died while visiting his son, Meriwether Lewis Clark, and was buried in St. Louis, where his funeral procession was a mile long.

Lewis's remaining years were not so happy. Always more passionate and accident-prone than his friend, he became governor of the Louisiana Territory and had nothing but problems administering the vast region that, largely thanks to his efforts, was now rapidly opening up.

In 1809 he heard from Washington that five hundred dollars he had charged up to official business would not be paid by the government. He was worried at the prospect of financial ruin, so he set off to

Silhouette of Meriwether Lewis by Dolley Madison

Meriwether Lewis

Folley

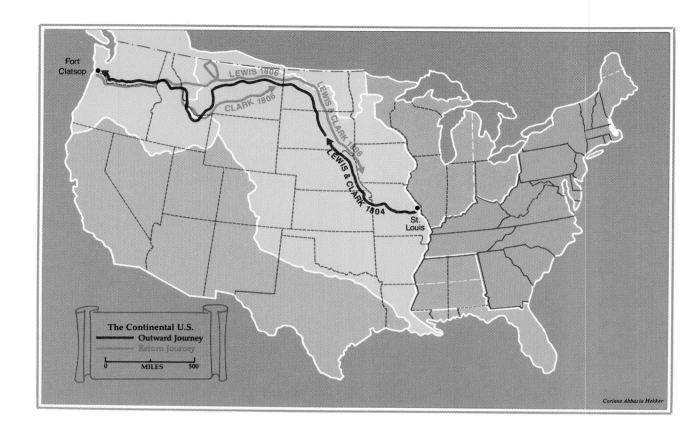

The Continental U.S.
Outward Journey
Return Journey

0 MILES 500

Corinne Abbazia Hekker

Washington to clear up the problem personally. When he arrived at Fort Pickering, near present-day Memphis, Tennessee, the post commander found him to be acting very strangely. He learned that the boat crew had been guarding Lewis constantly, because he had twice tried to commit suicide.

The party set off again, overland, down the Natchez trail, and on October 10 they stayed at Grinder's Stand, a couple of cabins and a stable in a clearing in the forest. Late that night, two shots were heard from Lewis's cabin. A moment later the explorer came staggering out, badly wounded. He collapsed at Mrs. Grinder's door, begging for help. Mrs. Grinder's husband was away, and she would not open the door. In the morning Lewis's servants found their master in his cabin, with terrible wounds to his head and side. A few hours later he died. Whether he was murdered by robbers or shot himself with his own gun remains a mystery. And so, at thirty-five, ended the life of the great explorer.

Finally, the romance that the expedition provides is one of its greatest legacies. The wild river, the grizzlies, the mountains, the Indian tribes—all are described in great detail in the captains' journals and form the stuff of pure adventure. It cannot be forgotten, however, that the adventure had consequences that were not all to the good. It was the Indians who paid the heaviest price for the American expansion that Lewis and Clark did so much to promote. Their sufferings in the decades that followed teach us that what was good for the white settlers was not necessarily good for the Indians. Lewis, Clark, Jefferson, and others might have liked to see the Indians fit into white civilization as peaceful farmers and trading partners, but it did not happen that way.

Still, Lewis and Clark and their men are true heroes in this adventure. They showed tremendous courage and intelligence in the face of sometimes bitterly hard conditions. They fulfilled the demanding instructions of their president and did a superior job not only as explorers but also as naturalists and diplomats. For all of this they are justly remembered.

INDEX

Page numbers in *italics* indicate illustrations

SUGGESTED READING

CUTRIGHT, PAUL R. *Lewis and Clark: Pioneering Naturalists.* Urbana, Ill.: University of Illinois Press, 1969.

DE VOTO, BERNARD, ed. *The Journals of Lewis and Clark.* Boston: Houghton Mifflin, 1953; reprinted 1963.

HOLLOWAY, DAVID. *Lewis and Clark and the Crossing of North America.* New York: Dutton, 1976.

JACKSON, DONALD D., ed. *Letters of the Lewis and Clark Expedition.* Urbana, Ill.: University of Illinois Press, 1962.

LACY, DAN. *The Lewis and Clark Expedition.* New York: Franklin Watts, 1974.

MAXWELL, JAMES A., ed. *America's Fascinating Indian Heritage.* Pleasantville, N.Y.: Reader's Digest, 1978.

SKOLD, BETTY W. *Sacagawea: The Story of an American Indian.* Minneapolis: Dillon Press, 1977.

SNYDER, GERALD S., and the NATIONAL GEOGRAPHIC SOCIETY. *In the Footsteps of Lewis and Clark.* Washington, D.C.: National Geographic Society, 1970.